ADVENTURES IN NATURE

# EXPLORING PARKS

BY JEN GREEN AND LIA VISIRIN

WINDMILL BOOKS

Published in 2026 by Windmill Books,
an Imprint of Rosen Publishing
2544 Clinton St.
Buffalo, NY 14224

First published in Great Britain in 2025 by Hodder & Stoughton


Credits
Series Editor: Julia Bird
Series Designer: Peter Scoulding

Cataloging-in-Publication Data
Names: Green, Jen, author. | Visirin, Lia, illustrator.
Title: Exploring parks / Jen Green, illustrated by Lia Visirin.
Description: Buffalo, NY : Windmill Books, 2026. | Series: Adventures in nature | Includes glossary and index.
Identifiers: ISBN 9781538398715 (pbk.) | ISBN 9781538398722 (library bound) | ISBN 9781538398739 (ebook)
Subjects: LCSH: Parks--Juvenile literature. | Nature study--Juvenile literature.
Classification: LCC SB481.3 G743 2026 | DDC 333.78'3--dc23



Printed in the United States of America

CPSIA Compliance Information: Batch #CSWM26
For Further Information contact Rosen Publishing at 1-800-237-9932

# CONTENTS

# IN THE PARK

Parks are green spaces, usually in built-up areas such as towns and cities. Some parks are huge, others are tiny. Big or small, parks provide a wild space for plants and animals to live. That's why parks are great places to study nature!

Parks contain thousands of different plants and animals, which you can discover if you look closely.

Animals in parks are often used to people. If you move slowly you can sometimes get quite close.

*This symbol warns when special care is needed. Always take good care of nature. Never pick plants and don't handle wild creatures.*

When looking for nature in the park, you will need warm, waterproof clothing, sneakers or boots, a hat, sunglasses, and sunscreen.

Make notes and drawings using a notebook, pen, and colored pencils. A magnifying glass, binoculars, phone camera, and a collecting jar can also be useful.

# PLACES TO LIVE

A habitat is a place where plants and animals live, such as a forest, lake, or meadow. Parks have different areas such as lawns, ponds, flowerbeds, and woodlands. Each is like a mini habitat with its own set of plants and animals.

Some parks have lawns and meadows. Red poppies and yellow dandelions are growing in this meadow.

These geese live on a pond where they can find food. They rest on its banks.

## WHAT DO YOU SEE?

You need to use your five senses and a little patience to explore nature. Take time to look and listen carefully. Be aware of smells and sounds. Keep still and quiet, so you don't scare animals away.

Bees and butterflies can be found near flowerbeds.

# CHANGING SEASONS

The park changes as the weather slowly gets warmer or colder. We call these changes the seasons. Plants and animals live their lives according to the yearly pattern of spring, summer, autumn, and winter. That means there's always something different to see in the park!

## WHAT DO YOU SEE?

Start to record what you see in the different seasons. Make notes and drawings of the changes in weather. Try to identify the plants and animals you see and record what the animals are doing.

Winter is the coldest season. Lakes and ponds can freeze over and snow may fall. Many trees have no leaves. Some animals spend winter asleep.

In spring the weather warms up. Trees and plants grow new leaves and blossoms. Birds build nests and lay their eggs. Young animals are born.

Summer is the warmest season. Leafy trees provide shade. Birds such as swans, and other animals rear their young (cygnets). Butterflies fly around.

In autumn the weather gets colder. Leaves turn yellow and fall from some types of trees. Animals such as squirrels prepare for winter by burying nuts to eat later.

**WHICH IS YOUR FAVORITE SEASON IN THE PARK?**

# IN THE GRASS

**Grassy lawns make great hiding places for wildflowers and minibeasts. Worms, beetles, and ants live in the soil. To a small creature such as an ant, the lawn is a towering jungle of green stalks, leaves, and flowers!**

Worms tunnel through the mud. They swallow soil and bits of plants.

Daisies open their petals during the day and close them at night. The word daisy is short for "day's eye."

## WHAT DO YOU SEE?

Ants scurry around finding food to take back to their nest. A long line of ants forms between the nest and the food. Follow the ant trail. Draw a map of the ants' route. What food have they found?

These ants are carrying supplies back to their home.

ANTS MAY BE RED, BLACK, OR YELLOW. WHAT COLOR ARE THE ONES YOU HAVE SEEN?

# IN THE TREES

Trees provide shade and a home for animals such as birds, squirrels, and minibeasts. Trees spread their leaves high in the air. The trunk supports the tree. The roots spread underground, gathering water.

Different species of trees have different shapes. Here are some common trees found in parks.

OAKS (RIGHT) AND CHESTNUTS (BELOW) HAVE A ROUNDED SHAPE.

FIR TREES HAVE A TRIANGULAR SHAPE.

POPLARS ARE TALL AND SLENDER.

Many different animals live in a big tree such as an oak. They can be found high on twigs and branches, on the bark, or hiding among the roots.

Trees have different shaped leaves. This can help you identify the tree. These are oak leaves.

HOW MANY DIFFERENT LEAF SHAPES CAN YOU FIND?

## WHAT DO YOU SEE?

Look for birds, squirrels, and butterflies high in trees using binoculars. What do you think the animals are doing? Can you identify the species you see?

Blackbirds are common woodland birds that sometimes nest in parks.

# IN A BUSH

Bushes and shrubs are smaller than trees, but share the same features: leaves, twigs, roots, and a woody stem. In spring and summer, all sorts of minibeasts make their homes in bushes. Some feed on leaves, while others hunt other bugs!

Leaves have lines called veins spreading out from their center. Veins carry food and water around the leaf.

These are some common minibeasts found in bushes.

CATERPILLARS ARE YOUNG BUTTERFLIES OR MOTHS.

APHIDS (RIGHT) - AND SHIELD BUGS (BELOW) SUCK PLANT SAP.

BARK BEETLES EAT LEAVES. THEIR YOUNG EAT WOOD.

HOW MANY DIFFERENT MINIBEASTS CAN YOU FIND?

Spiders spin their webs in bushes to catch prey such as flies.

## WHAT DO YOU SEE?

Investigate the minibeasts that live in a bush. Spread a sheet or tablecloth under the bush. Gently shake a branch and see what lands on the sheet. Look at your finds using a magnifying glass.

Butterflies visit buddleja flowers to sip sugary nectar.

# BY THE WATER

Water in a park includes rivers, streams, and ponds. Many living things are found by water. As well as plants such as reeds and lilies, there are waterbirds, dragonflies, fish, and frogs.

These waterbirds are common in parks.

A MOORHEN HAS A RED BEAK.

A COOT HAS A WHITE PATCH ABOVE THE BILL.

THIS GULL HAS A BLACK HEAD.

Dragonflies grow up underwater. The adult insects live on land and hunt for food while flying.

***Be careful near water. Stay close to a trusted adult and don't go too close to the edge.***

Male mallard ducks have a blue and green head and gray, brown, and black feathers. Female mallards have speckled brown feathers. Both have a blue patch on their wing.

## WHAT DO YOU SEE?

Look for waterbirds using your binoculars. Ducks, swans, geese, and gulls swim in open water. Coots and moorhens lurk around the edge. Can you identify the birds you see?

CAN YOU SPOT WHAT THE WATERBIRDS ARE DOING IN YOUR PARK?

# UNDER A STONE

All sorts of minibeasts live under stones and in damp corners. Counting their legs can help you identify them. Insects such as beetles and earwigs have six legs. Spiders have eight. Centipedes, millipedes, and woodlice have many legs. Slugs, snails, and worms have no legs.

This is a centipede.

These creepy-crawlies are found under stones.

A GROUND BEETLE HUNTS SMALLER MINIBEASTS.

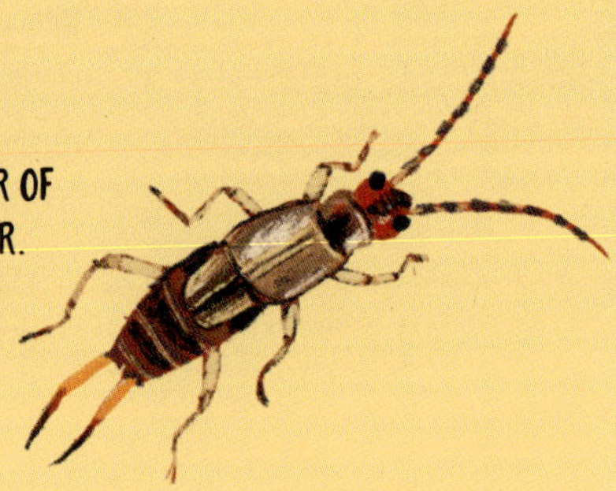

AN EARWIG HAS A PAIR OF PINCERS ON ITS REAR.

A WOODLOUSE HAS AN ARMOR-PLATED BODY.

## WHAT DO YOU SEE?

Turn over a stone carefully to see what minibeasts live beneath. Count their legs to identify them.

*Watch out – minibeasts can bite! Always wash your hands after touching soil.*

A snail's shell protects its soft body.

Slugs move along by squeezing the muscles in their long, flat foot.

HOW CAN YOU TELL THE DIFFERENCE BETWEEN SLUGS AND SNAILS?

# FLOWERS

**Flowers brighten up the park and provide food for insects. Their sweet scent and bright colors attract bees and butterflies. As insects fly between flowers, they transfer dusty pollen. This allows flowers to make seeds, so new plants can grow.**

## WHAT DO YOU SEE?

Try drawing the flowers you see. First study the petals' shape. Some petals are flat or rounded, others are shaped like stars or bells. Add color with pencils or pens.

Flowers have different shapes and colors, but all have the same parts: a stem, petals, and long stalks called stamens that produce pollen.

Bees visit flowers to sip nectar. A bee's body is dusted with pollen, which rubs off on the next flower it visits. This allows the second flower to make seeds.

Flowers bloom at different times of year.

CROCUSES BLOOM IN SPRING.

IRISES BLOOM IN SUMMER.

PANSIES CAN BLOOM IN SPRING, SUMMER, AUTUMN, OR WINTER.

**WHAT INSECTS DO YOU SEE VISITING FLOWERS?**

Tulips bloom in spring. Their cup-shaped flowers open during the day and close at night.

# LIFE CYCLES

**If you visit a park often, you will see small changes taking place from day to day. In just a few days, flowers bloom, then drop their petals and make seeds. After a few weeks, young insects hatch from eggs and grow into adults. These changes are part of life cycles.**

Weeds called dandelions have a speedy life cycle. In just a day or two, the flower opens, blooms, and dies.

After the flower dies, winged seeds form. The wind blows the seeds away.

Butterflies have a four-stage life cycle. In spring, the adults lay eggs, which hatch into caterpillars. The fully grown caterpillar turns into a pupa. Inside the pupa case it transforms again into a butterfly.

## WHAT DO YOU SEE?

Look for caterpillars in spring and summer. Look on the underside of leaves that have been nibbled. Each caterpillar has a favorite food plant. Can you identify the plant?

***Never touch caterpillars, as they may have hairs that can sting.***

# FOOD CHAINS

**Living things in a park form a web of life. The links between them can be shown in diagrams called food chains. Plants are at the base of most food chains. They make their own food using sunlight energy, water, and minerals from the soil. Plants provide food for animals called herbivores. These are hunted by meat-eating predators.**

This food chain shows the links between a ladybug, aphid, and rose. The ladybug is at the top of this chain.

Aphids are often found eating roses. Ladybugs hunt aphids, which helps to save the flowers!

This robin is eating a mealworm – a young beetle. Mealworms feed on young plants.

## WHAT DO YOU SEE?

Draw a food chain showing the robin, mealworm, and plants. Now try drawing other simple food chains that you see in the park. You will need to know what each animal eats.

# DAY BY DAY

Animals in the park follow a daily rhythm. Some are out and about by day, like humans. Others search for food at dawn, dusk, or at night. For example, butterflies gather nectar early in the morning. Most birds look for food during the day. Moths and bats fly at night.

Squirrels are active during the daytime, looking for nuts, seeds, and fruit.

## WHAT DO YOU SEE?

Visit a park at different times of day – for example in the early morning, at midday, and dusk. Record the animals that are active in trees, on the grass, and by the water, if there are any.

Birds sing at dawn. This is called the dawn chorus.

Shy animals such as foxes, mice, and hedgehogs look for food in the dark.

# NATURE DIARY

Build up a picture of life in a park by keeping a nature diary. A wildlife book or website can help you identify plants and animals. You could collect finds such as leaves and even draw a map of the park.

## KEEP NOTES

Always take your notebook with you. Record the date, time, weather, and place. Describe what you see. Add drawings and photos to illustrate your book.

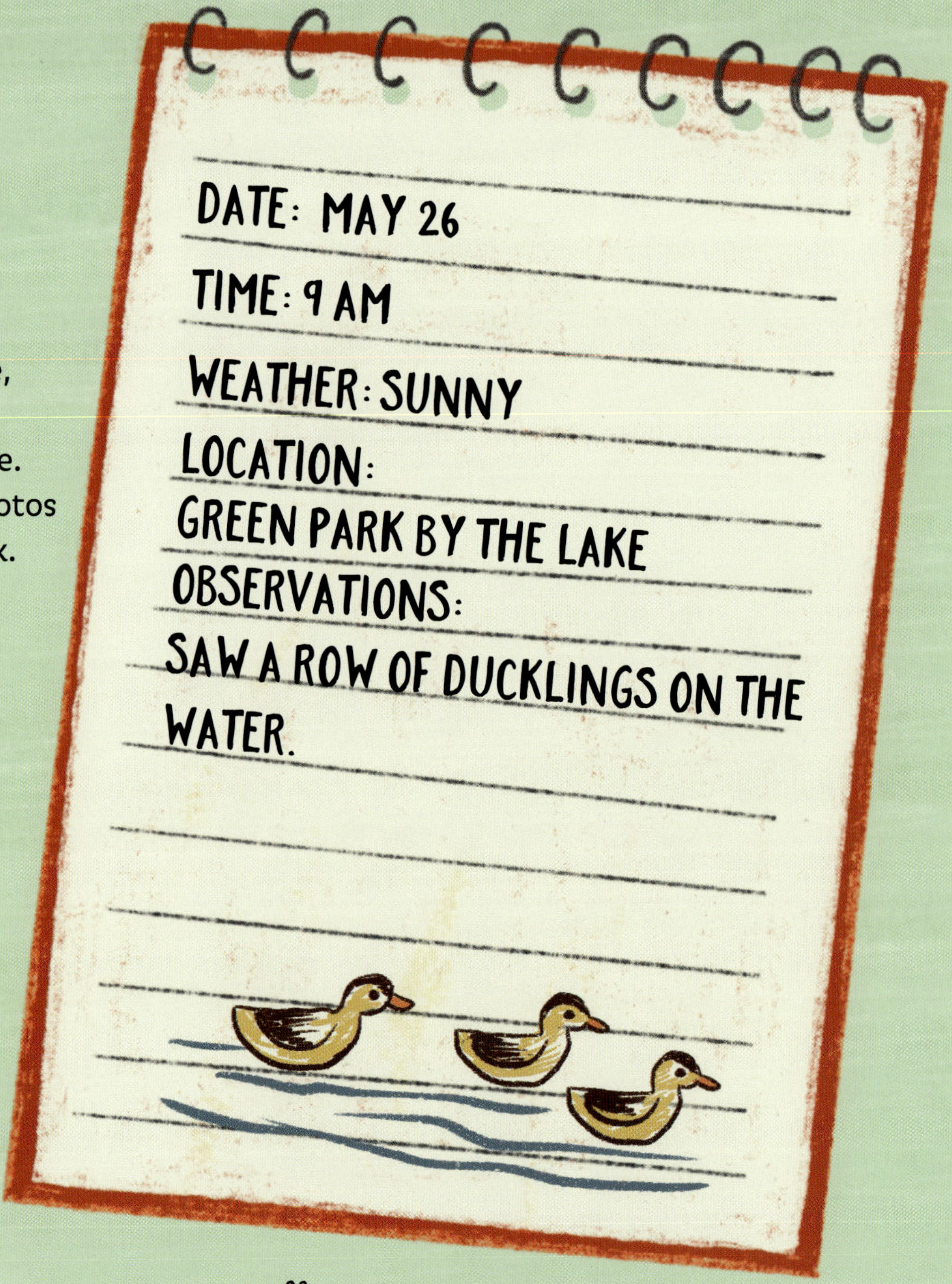

You could collect leaves, nuts, seeds, and feathers to stick in your diary, or create tree rubbings.

What insect is this? If you don't recognize a plant or animal, make a quick sketch or take a photo. Look it up later online or in a plant or animal book.

## TOP TIPS

- Don't forget to keep still and quiet when you go nature-spotting.
- Try not to let your shadow fall on animals such as insects, as it will scare them away.
- Approach animals with the wind blowing toward you so they don't catch your scent.

## MAKE A MAP

Make a map of the park showing mini-habitats such as trees, lawns, wild areas, lakes, and flowerbeds. Show paths and buildings too.

# GLOSSARY

**Armor-plated** when an insect or animal has a hard, protective shell.

**Bloom** when flowering plants come into flower. This usually happens in the spring or summer.

**Bush** a woody plant that is smaller than a tree.

**Habitat** the natural home of a plant or animal, such as a wood, meadow, or pond.

**Herbivore** an animal that eats plants.

**Location** a place.

**Nectar** a sweet, sugary liquid produced by flowers to attract insects.

**Petals** the brightly colored parts of a flower, similar to leaves.

**Pincers** moveable parts of some insects that are used to pick up and carry things.

**Pollen** yellow grains produced by flowers in order to make seeds.

**Predator** an animal that hunts other animals for food.

**Prey** an animal that is hunted by another.

**Pupa** the third stage in the life cycle of a moth or butterfly, before it becomes an adult.

**Shrub** a woody plant that is smaller than a tree.

**Species** a type of plant or animal, such as an oak tree or a tortoiseshell butterfly.

**Stamens** the long stalks in the middle of a flower that produce pollen.

**Veins** lines that run through leaves, supplying water and food.

# FIND OUT MORE

**Books**

*Nature's Classroom: Birds* by Izzi Howell, Wayland, 2023

*Bugs Save the World* by Buglife, Wayland, 2022

*Nature Needs You* by Liz Gogerly, Franklin Watts, 2021

**Websites**

*www.wildlifewatch.org.uk/*
The Wildlife Watch website is packed with facts about birds, mammals, and other wildlife.

*www.bbc.co.uk/springwatch/*
*www.bbc.co.uk/autumnwatch/*
The BBC's Springwatch and Autumnwatch sites have information about exploring the natural world.

*https://www.allaboutbirds.org/news/best-bird-sounds-audio-macaulay-library-2025/*
Listen to different birdsong and wildlife sounds.

# INDEX